A fish for Jamila

On the water are some …

The mother looked for fish.

No fish!

Jamila had some cake.
Have some cake!

Cake is good.

Jamila went off to school.

I gave it some cake, Mr Belter.
Kick the ball, Kevin!

School is for children, not for you!
Get it out!

Jamila was painting.

Go away!
Off you go!

It went to the water.

But on the way home ...

Cake is good!

I have no cake.
I gave you all my cake.
No cake!

No cake!

The mother splashed into the water.

Have a fish!